Malaria

Rachel Lynette

KIDHAVEN PRESS

An imprint of Thomson Gale, a part of The Thomson Corporation

THOMSON

™

GALE

Detroit • New York • San Francisco • San Diego • New Haven, Conn. • Waterville, Maine • London • Munich

LIBRARY OF CONGRESS CATALOGING-IN-PUBLICATION DATA

Lynette, Rachel.
  Malaria / by Rachel Lynette.
    p. cm. — (Understanding diseases and disorders)
  Includes bibliographical references and index.
  Contents: A devastating disease—The causes and spread of malaria—
    When malaria strikes—Preventing and treating malaria.
  ISBN 0-7377-2641-5 (hard cover : alk. paper)
  1. Malaria—Juvenile literature. I. Title. II. Series.
  RC157.L965 2005
  616.9'362—dc22

                                                        2005001677

Printed in the United States of America

Contents

Chapter 1
A Devastating Disease   4

Chapter 2
The Causes and Spread of Malaria   12

Chapter 3
When Malaria Strikes   20

Chapter 4
Preventing and Treating Malaria   29

Notes   40

Glossary   42

For Further Exploration   44

Index   46

Picture Credits   48

About the Author   48

Chapter One

A Devastating Disease

Malaria is a serious illness that affects millions of people every year. In a typical case of malaria, the first symptoms are tiredness and chills followed by a high fever. The fever may be accompanied by other flulike symptoms, such as body aches, headache, nausea, vomiting, and joint pain. These symptoms usually subside after four to six hours but will recur every two or three days. Within one to four weeks, the attacks end and the victim recovers. In some people, however, the disease will **relapse**, or return. A person with relapsing malaria may have occasional bouts of the disease throughout his or her lifetime.

Many people get infected with a more severe form of malaria. This type of malaria can affect the brain and nervous system, causing confusion, seizures, and coma. The liver and spleen may be damaged, and the victim's kidneys may fail. The victim may also develop anemia, a weakened state caused when a person has too few red blood cells. One out of every four people who contract this kind of malaria will die. Those who do not die may be left with serious health problems, such as difficulty in moving and speaking, deafness, and blindness.

A woman in a hospital in Sudan, Africa, cradles her infant son who suffers from malaria, a very serious disease.

Christine Zulu, a nurse in Zambia, describes her experience with malaria:

> We were working on a patient when suddenly, I felt very cold. I tried to continue but was seized by violent shivering and goose pimples broke out all over me. My temperature had risen to 38.5 degrees Celsius (101.3 Fahrenheit) and my joints were painful. I was restless and couldn't breathe properly. I tried to help with a patient and almost fell over her. At that moment, I knew I was very ill.[1]

Zulu's malaria became even more serious. By the next day she could not walk and did not recognize her sister when she came to visit. Zulu fell into a coma that lasted two days, during which she nearly died. On the third day, she awoke unable to hear or speak. She eventually made a full recovery, but it took over a month.

Who Gets Malaria?

About 40 percent of the world's population is at risk of getting malaria. Most of these people live in poor countries with hot climates. More than 300 million people in these countries get malaria every year and about a million people die from the disease. Ninety percent of these deaths occur in Africa, and most of the victims are children under the age of five. Every day 3,000 children in Africa die of malaria, which is one child every 30 seconds. Pregnant women are also at high risk for getting malaria. When a preg-

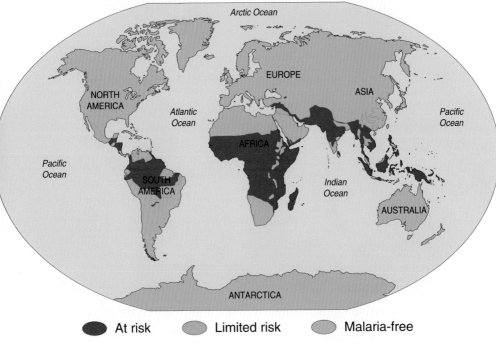

Areas Most at Risk for Malaria

Arctic Ocean

EUROPE

NORTH
AMERICA

ASIA

Atlantic
Ocean

Pacific
Ocean

AFRICA

Pacific
Ocean

SOUTH
AMERICA

Indian
Ocean

AUSTRALIA

ANTARCTICA

● At risk   ○ Limited risk   ○ Malaria-free

Source: World Health Organization, 2003.

nant woman contracts the disease, both she and the fetus can suffer serious health problems or even die.

Although most cases of malaria today are found in underdeveloped countries, it used to be a world-wide problem. Malaria has stricken people in almost every corner of the world. In some societies, **epidemics** of malaria were so widespread that they changed the course of history.

An Ancient Disease

Malaria may be the oldest disease in human history. Many scientists believe that malaria has been around as long as humans have. Outbreaks of malaria-like illnesses have been noted from as early as 6000 B.C.

In this historical painting, a family of French peasants infected with malaria sails along a river, far from all human contact.

Malaria began in Africa and spread throughout Asia and Europe. It was common in ancient Rome (27 B.C.–A.D. 378) and may even have contributed to the empire's downfall. Scientists have found evidence of malaria in human bones from that time period. Most agree that malaria was a serious problem in ancient Rome. Some historians believe malaria might even have weakened the Roman army and contributed to the disappearance of whole villages.

Malaria spread throughout Europe and into North and South America. One reason why malaria spread so quickly was because people did not know what caused the disease. It was this lack of knowledge that resulted in thousands of deaths in Panama in the late 1800s when the French tried and failed to build a canal there.

Malaria and the Panama Canal

When the French began construction on a canal in 1880, they did not know that malaria is spread by mosquitoes. Mosquitoes thrive in hot climates and lay their eggs in small pools of standing water. Panama's tropical weather and long rainy season made it the perfect place for the mosquitoes that spread malaria. Since the French did not know that the mosquitoes were dangerous, they made no attempt to exterminate them. In fact, they often unknowingly did things that made the problem even worse. In hospitals, nurses routinely put the legs of beds into buckets of water to stop other insects from crawling up them and onto patients. These buckets of water made ideal breeding places for the mosquitoes. Many patients came to the hospital with minor injuries only to die there a few weeks later from malaria. Over 20,000 workers and family members died during the French occupation of Panama. Many of them died of malaria, contributing to France's failure to complete the canal.

In the early 1900s, America decided to attempt to build a canal in Panama. By this time, the link between mosquitoes and malaria had been discovered. William Gorgas, the man in charge of the effort to rid the canal zone of disease, knew what to do to fight malaria. He had screens put on the doors and windows of houses and other buildings, and he had the insides fumigated, or sprayed with **insecticide.** Kerosene oil was dumped on swamps, ponds, and puddles to kill the mosquitoes and their eggs. People were ordered to cover pitchers, pots, and other water containers. Ridding the canal zone of mosquitoes was expensive, but in the end it worked. Malaria did not become a major problem for the Americans, and the canal was completed in 1913.

Malaria Today

In 1955 the World Health Organization (WHO) launched a nearly worldwide program to eliminate malaria. The insecticide **DDT** (dichloro-diphenyl-trichloroethane) was used to kill the mosquitoes that carry malaria in cooler countries where the mosquitoes cannot live all year long. As a result, malaria was wiped out in most of Europe and in all of the United States.

Today virtually all cases of malaria in the United States involve people who have gotten the disease

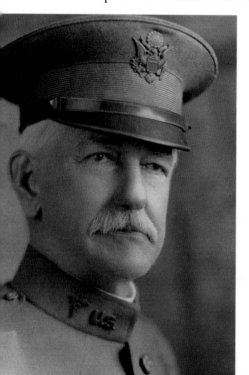

William Gorgas wiped out mosquito populations near the Panama Canal to help control the spread of malaria.

In 1958 a worker for the National Malaria Eradication Program sprays DDT over a swamp to kill mosquitoes.

while visiting countries where malaria is a problem. There are about 1,200 cases a year in the United States. Since malaria cannot be spread from person to person, these cases are usually isolated.

DDT was also used in some warmer countries, where it helped to reduce cases of malaria, but it could not wipe it out completely. Sub-Saharan Africa was not included in the WHO plan because it was believed the program would not work in an area with so few resources. Because they were not destroyed, the mosquito population in Africa continued to grow. As a result, today malaria remains a serious problem in sub-Saharan Africa, killing three times as many people as it did 30 years ago.

Chapter Two

The Causes and Spread of Malaria

Hippocrates, the Greek physician known as "the Father of Medicine," noticed that outbreaks of a disease historians believe was malaria often occurred near marshes in warm and humid weather. In fact, the word *malaria* means "bad air" in Italian.

The first person to actually see the **parasite** that causes malaria was Alphonse Laveran, a French army surgeon stationed in Algeria in 1880. Using a microscope, he saw the parasite in the blood of a patient suffering from malaria. A few years later the mystery of how the disease was spread was solved by Ronald Ross, a British officer in the Indian Medical Service. In 1897 Ross found the malaria parasite in the stomach of a mosquito that had bitten a person with malaria a few days earlier. He realized that the parasite could be spread to humans by mosquitoes.

The Types of Malaria Parasites

Scientists today know that there are four different types of Plasmodium parasites that cause malaria: Plasmodium falciparum, Plasmodium vivax, Plasmodium ovale, and Plasmodium malariae. Each of these parasites causes a different kind of malaria. Plasmodium falciparum causes the deadliest kind of malaria, killing millions of people every year, most of them children. Plasmodium vivax and Plasmodium ovale are rarely fatal, but they can cause relapses

In 1897 Ronald Ross discovered that mosquitoes carry the malaria parasite and spread the disease through their bites.

of the disease. This is because these parasites have a **dormant** stage that can last months or even years. People with these kinds of malaria may think that they have recovered, only to get sick again. The final kind of parasite, Plasmodium malariae, is also rarely fatal, but it can exist inside a person without causing symptoms for many years or even a whole lifetime.

The Parasite Life Cycle

Plasmodium parasites have a complicated life cycle. They must inhabit two different **hosts**: female Anopheles mosquitoes and humans. When a person

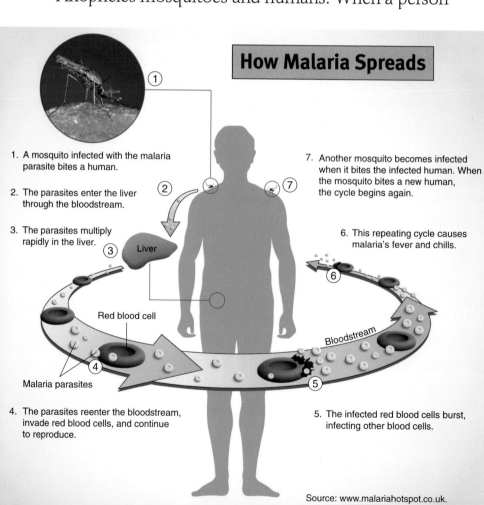

How Malaria Spreads

1. A mosquito infected with the malaria parasite bites a human.

2. The parasites enter the liver through the bloodstream.

3. The parasites multiply rapidly in the liver.

Liver

Red blood cell

Malaria parasites

4. The parasites reenter the bloodstream, invade red blood cells, and continue to reproduce.

7. Another mosquito becomes infected when it bites the infected human. When the mosquito bites a new human, the cycle begins again.

6. This repeating cycle causes malaria's fever and chills.

Bloodstream

5. The infected red blood cells burst, infecting other blood cells.

Source: www.malariahotspot.co.uk.

is bitten by an infected female Anopheles mosquito, the Plasmodium parasites make their way to the victim's liver through the bloodstream. This takes less than half an hour. The parasites then spend ten to fourteen days in the liver reproducing. Each cell divides in half to make two individual cells. The parasites do this thousands of times. During this period, the victim does not have any symptoms. The parasites then leave the liver and reenter the bloodstream, where they invade red blood cells and continue to reproduce until the cells burst. The parasites continue to invade more blood cells, which makes the victim sick. The victim's temperature begins to rise, and he or she shows other signs of malaria.

If a person sick with malaria is bitten by a female Anopheles mosquito, some parasites will be sucked up by the mosquito along with the blood. Once inside the mosquito, the parasites make their way to the mosquito's gut, where they spend two to three weeks reproducing. The parasites then return to the mosquito's salivary glands. When the mosquito bites another person, the parasites enter the person's bloodstream and the whole cycle begins again.

The Anopheles Mosquito

The reason the parasites that cause malaria are dangerous is because of the insect that spreads them— the Anopheles mosquito. There are 430 known species of Anopheles mosquitoes, 30 to 50 of which can spread malaria. These mosquitoes can be found in all but the coldest climates. They are especially plentiful in hot, humid places, such as many parts of Asia and Africa.

Female Anopheles mosquitoes bite people because they need the energy that blood gives them in order to lay their eggs. A single Anopheles mosquito will lay between 50 and 200 eggs at a time. They must lay their eggs in small bodies of standing water, which are common in malaria-ridden countries. According to Melanie Renshaw of the United Nations Children's Fund, who runs anti-malarial operations in Mozambique, "There are marshes, creeks and pools of standing water everywhere. The shanty houses are put together from all sorts of materials, so there are plenty of spots where mosquitoes can get in and hide."[2]

The water must be warm for the eggs to hatch. In colder places, the eggs may lie dormant in the winter and hatch in the spring, but in hot climates the eggs can hatch after about a week. This means that mosquitoes in warm climates can breed all year long.

Skillful Hunters

Anopheles mosquitoes are skilled hunters. They typically bite at night and are most active during the twilight hours. The mosquitoes cannot see very well, but they are attracted to motion. They also have an excellent sense of smell and can detect human sweat from more than 60 feet (18 meters) away. In addition, these mosquitoes can use their anten-

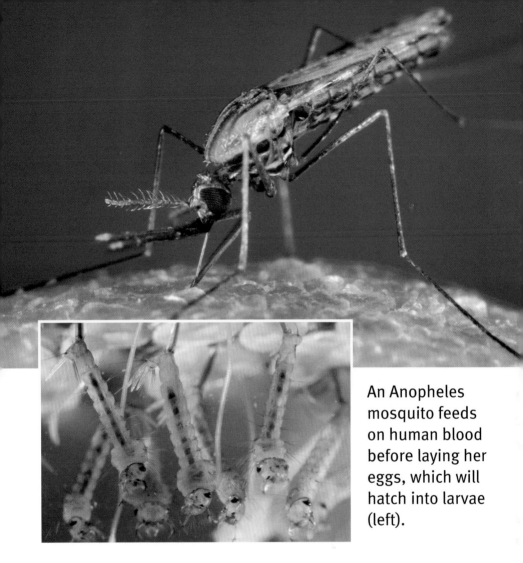

An Anopheles mosquito feeds on human blood before laying her eggs, which will hatch into larvae (left).

nas to sense the heat given off by people's bodies. A single female Anopheles mosquito may bite several people before laying her eggs. This is why a whole family can sometimes come down with malaria all at once.

Malaria Is on the Rise

Countries with many cases of malaria may experience even more outbreaks when the environment

A child in Mozambique, Africa, plays in a stagnant pool of water, an ideal breeding ground for mosquitoes.

is favorable to the mosquitoes that spread it. Since mosquitoes need water to breed, tropical countries with rainy seasons usually see an increase of malaria during these times. Earthquakes and hurricanes can also cause malaria outbreaks. Widespread destruction often leads to poor sanitation and crowded shelters for survivors, both of which attract mosquitoes.

Another reason for increasing cases of malaria in developing countries is development itself. When forests are cut down to make room for cities and industry, rainwater collects in puddles on the now bare ground, attracting mosquitoes. Mosquitoes are also attracted to muddy construction sites where water is used to make cement and bricks. Irrigation systems, sewers, and dams provide even more breeding grounds. Cases of malaria often increase in areas where there is a lot of construction.

Mosquitoes are difficult to control, mainly because there are so many of them and they can breed even in very small bodies of water—water in a flower vase or a leftover beverage can, for example. But controlling or at least avoiding female Anopheles mosquitoes is an essential part of the fight against malaria.

Chapter Three

When Malaria Strikes

Although malaria is a problem for many countries with tropical climates, the situation is worse in sub-Saharan Africa and some parts of Asia. In these countries, cases of malaria are high, especially during the rainy seasons, and severe malaria is common. In addition, even when a person makes a full recovery, he or she is still in danger of getting the disease again.

Malaria's Victims

One of the tragic things about malaria is that it is most likely to strike children under age five and pregnant women. Adults who have had malaria several times and have survived it are less likely to get malaria. And even if they do get it, the symptoms will be less severe. This is because they have been exposed to the parasite many times and their bodies have learned to fight it off. This is called **immunity**. Children under five have not built up immunity to the disease and so are most at risk. They are also smaller and weaker than adults. According to Jose Stoute, a doctor who works at a hospital in Kenya, "Children here are repeatedly exposed to one bout of malaria after another after another after another."[3] Stoute says that as much as 80 percent of the local population in Kenya may be infected with malaria.

Children in sub-Saharan Africa are also at risk because the mosquitoes in this part of the world

A woman in a Sudan hospital comforts her five-year-old son, who is suffering from a severe case of malaria.

carry Plasmodium falciparum, the most severe form of malaria. Jack Chow, the assistant director general of the World Health Organization's AIDS, tuberculosis, and malaria section, explains: "When the malaria parasite begins to infect children, it has an even harsher effect on their health compared to an adult. Many children have neurological [nerve and brain] damage from . . . malaria and they live with that . . . damage for the rest of their lives."[4] This damage can include poor mental functioning, paralysis, deafness, and blindness.

The risks for pregnant women who get malaria are also great. Although a woman may have built

Many children in sub-Saharan Africa, like this boy in Mozambique, are infected with malaria.

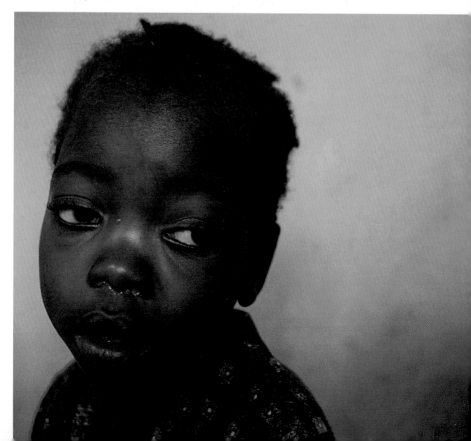

up immunity to malaria during her lifetime, this immunity decreases during pregnancy. Women who get malaria while they are pregnant may suffer from illnesses that can harm the fetus. About 10,000 pregnant women die from malaria every year in sub-Saharan Africa, leaving any children they already have without a mother. Those who survive may have babies who are born too early or have low birth weights. Babies with low birth weights are likely to be mentally disabled or to have other serious health problems. Each year 75,000 to 200,000 infants in Africa die from problems due to maternal malaria.

How Malaria Harms Families

When malaria strikes, it has a devastating effect. Malaria often causes serious financial hardships. Adults may miss work because they are sick or must care for a sick child. This leads to missed wages or even the loss of a much-needed job. It could also mean that crops are not cared for or harvested if the family earns its living by farming. According to the Malaria Foundation, a single bout of malaria will cost a person ten to twenty missed days of work.

There are also other costs resulting from malaria. The drugs used to treat malaria often cost more than a poor family can afford. Traveling to clinics to see doctors adds to the burden. If problems arise, hospital care and treatments must be paid for. If the patient dies, the family will need to pay for the burial.

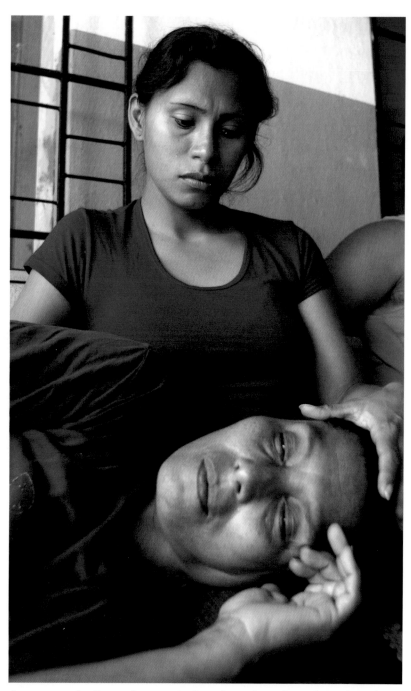

A woman in Ecuador rests her head on her daughter's lap as she waits for the results of a malaria test.

If the victim was an adult, children may be left with no one to care for them and no one to earn money for the family.

Bizunesh Tekom lives in Ethiopia. She and her children all contracted malaria during an epidemic that hit her town during the summer of 2003. "My husband has died. I have four children. What can a wife and children do alone?"[5] she asks. Bizunesh cannot afford to be sick. Her small savings are gone, and she must be healthy enough to farm her small plot of land and sell her vegetables. She is worried about the time that she is sick in the hospital and about how she will feed and care for her sick children with no one to help her.

Emotional Impact

Although the financial hardships of coping with malaria can be measured, there is no way to measure the huge emotional toll that malaria takes on families. In an article in the *New York Times,* Nicholas D. Kristof tells the story of Yok Yorn, a father in Cambodia who lost his seven-year-old son, Kaiset, to malaria. Yorn had carried his son to the doctor a week earlier. He borrowed money for the doctor's fee, which was much more than he could afford. But Kaiset had severe malaria and could not be saved. Kaiset was Yorn's second son to die from the disease. Yorn has five more children, but this does not comfort him as his family sobs over Kaiset's body. "I'm so afraid that my other children will die of malaria as well,"[6] says Yorn.

Malaria in Bermi

Outbreaks of malaria can have a serious effect on communities. The people of the small farming village of Bermi in northern Tanzania call malaria their biggest problem. They have devoted some of their Web site to describing how malaria has affected their community. Malaria has even made the creation of the Web site difficult. According to the site, which was written by many villagers, "If a group of five are to meet to discuss the Web site, on any given day one or two will be suffering from malaria and two others will be busy looking after relatives, or family, suffering with malaria."[7]

The site goes on to say, "With the rainy season, malaria has become a serious problem for us. From February to May, every household has been affected and many children have died."[8] Children in Bermi get malaria an average of five times a year. It costs a family 75 percent of its annual income to treat one child over the course of a year, and most families have more than one child.

These frequent bouts of malaria take a heavy toll on the village:

> Because most of us are sick, we are unable to work on developing our village. The mothers are in the hospital all day looking after their children and their husbands are too busy preparing food for the children to work.

A family in Liberia waits in a malaria clinic with their infected daughter. Clinics across Africa are overwhelmed with malaria patients.

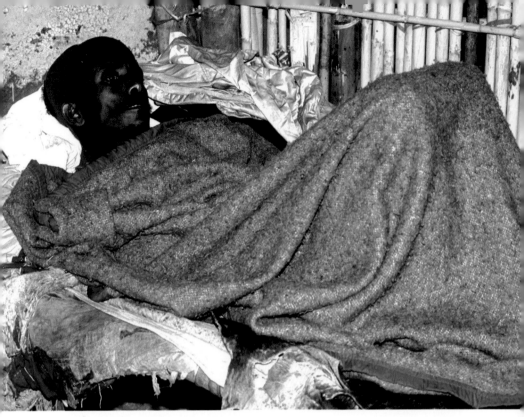

A malaria patient in Ethiopia is confined to his bed. Too sick to work, he cannot earn money to support his family.

> When malaria hits a family they are unable to earn any money; but they have very large hospital bills to pay. We wish to buy mosquito nets for every family, but the village has no money.[9]

Bermi's situation is not unique. Villages all across Africa are facing similar challenges. Some villages are lucky. Charitable organizations supply them with mosquito nets and medical care. For these villages, there is some hope of ending the cycle of poverty and disease.

Chapter Four

Preventing and Treating Malaria

Malaria has become such a big problem in Africa and some parts of Asia that the World Health Organization (WHO) has determined that wiping out the disease is not possible. Instead, WHO hopes to control the disease by creating a global partnership between organizations such as the United Nations Children's Fund (UNICEF), the World Bank, governments, communities, and private organizations. In 1998 more than 90 organizations united to form the Roll Back Malaria (RBM) campaign. The campaign's mission is to cut the amount of malaria in half by 2010.

Roll Back Malaria is using several strategies to achieve this goal. It educates local communities about what they can do to prevent malaria. It also trains health care workers to identify and treat

Children in Papua New Guinea sit beneath a net treated with insecticide. Few families in poor countries are able to afford these nets.

malaria. In addition, it provides much-needed anti-malarial drugs, medical equipment, insecticide spray, and bed nets to communities in epidemic areas.

Preventing Malaria

The best way to avoid getting malaria is to avoid getting bitten by mosquitoes that carry the disease. Health officials are focusing on two highly effective mosquito-prevention methods.

The first strategy is getting people (especially children under age five and pregnant women) to sleep under insecticide-treated mosquito nets. Health officials have found that deaths from malaria can be reduced by 50 percent in communities where most of the people sleep under these nets. However, health workers face several challenges. The nets cost about five dollars each, which is more than most families in underdeveloped countries can afford. They must also be treated with insecticide at least once a year to remain effective.

According to Bernard Muthaka of the Bamburi Health Centre in Mombasa, Kenya, "There is a high level of knowledge that malaria is caused by mosquitoes and a good percentage of people know

A boy in Senegal wears a miniature net on his head to help protect his skin from mosquito bites.

about sleeping under insecticide treated nets. However, the coverage of mosquito nets even in areas endemic to malaria [where the disease is very common] is still low, exposing huge populations to the disease."[10] There are many organizations trying to solve this problem by bringing nets to communities at low cost or free of charge.

A second strategy that health care workers are using is widespread insecticide spraying of indoor spaces. This method is effective when done correctly. There are some challenges, however. Buildings must be sprayed regularly and thoroughly to assure protection. An effective, inexpensive, and safe insecticide must be used. Some insecticides, including DDT, have been found to be dangerous to

To help control the spread of malaria, a worker in a refugee camp in Tanzania sprays a house with insecticide.

A man poses near a cinchona tree in the Amazon Rainforest. He will harvest the bark, from which an antimalarial drug called quinine will be extracted.

people, animals, and the environment. These insecticides are banned in some countries. Like the nets, in order for indoor spraying to work, it must be provided free of charge or at a very low cost.

Controlling mosquitoes is a difficult job. Despite the efforts of individuals, communities, and organizations such as RBM, millions of people are still being bitten by infected mosquitoes and are getting malaria. These people need fast, effective treatment.

Treating Malaria

Most cases of malaria are treated at home with oral antimalarial drugs. These drugs work by stopping the growth of the parasite. The drugs are most effective if the treatment is begun within 24 hours of the first symptoms. **Quinine** has been used to fight malaria since the early seventeenth century. Quinine comes from the bark of the cinchona tree, which is native to South America. Quinine is still used today because it is inexpensive and effective. However, it does have some serious side effects. People who take quinine often experience nausea, headaches, temporary hearing loss, and blurred vision. In most cases, quinine should be taken for seven days. Symptoms of malaria usually lessen within two to three days after the first dose.

There are several other drugs that are used to fight malaria. Some of these are too expensive to use in developing countries, and others are no longer used because of harmful side effects. Drugs such as mefloquine and artemisinin are often used in combination with each other or with antibiotics to improve their effectiveness.

In cases of severe malaria, the patient should be hospitalized if possible and given quinine **intravenously**. The patient may also have to be treated for problems related to the illness.

Challenges in the Fight Against Malaria

Poverty is a big challenge to fighting malaria in developing countries. But there are other challenges, too. One of the most difficult problems is that many of the methods used to fight malaria in the past no longer work.

Mosquitoes have become resistant to DDT and other common insecticides. When an area is sprayed with insecticide, a small percentage of the mosquitoes do not die, either because they were not exposed to enough of the insecticide to kill them or because something in their body chemistry makes them immune. These mosquitoes breed and pass their resistance to the insecticide on to their offspring. After a while most of the mosquitoes in the area are resistant to the insecticide. People combat this problem by using more of the insecticide and by developing new insecticides.

A boy in Indonesia covers his nose for protection as a man sprays an insecticide to kill mosquito populations.

A more serious problem than mosquitoes becoming resistant to insecticides is malaria parasites becoming resistant to antimalarial drugs. Often people who get malaria stop taking the antimalarial drug when their symptoms go away. Even though they no longer have symptoms, these people might not have gotten rid of all the malaria parasites in their bodies. The parasites that remain are stronger than the ones that were killed with the first few doses of the drug. These stronger parasites then reproduce, creating more strong parasites that are less likely to be killed by antimalarial drugs.

Drug resistance is a major factor in the increase of malaria deaths over the last few decades. Unfortu-

A nurse in Kenya prepares drugs for malaria patients. Unfortunately, malaria parasites are growing resistant to many drugs.

nately, the parasite Plasmodium falciparum, which causes the most severe type of malaria, has developed resistance to nearly all of the currently available anti-malarial drugs. The newest drug, artemisinin, is still effective, especially when combined with other drugs. But scientists expect the parasite to show resistance to the drug by the end of this decade.

The Future of Malaria

Wiping out malaria in the near future is highly unlikely. However, there is some hope that the disease can be controlled and that cases of malaria, especially in young children, will decrease. Scientists are researching new ways to control mosquitoes and new drugs to treat malaria.

Some of the most promising research focuses on developing a **vaccine** for malaria. Several vaccines have been developed and are being tested. The one that has worked the best attacks the parasite while it is still in the liver. Researchers from the University of Barcelona in Spain have tested the vaccine on 2,022 children in Mozambique. They found that the vaccine cut the number of cases of severe malaria by 58 percent. Lead researcher Pedro Alonso says it is not realistic to expect any vaccine to be 100 percent effective: "It's difficult to imagine that we will have in the near future a magic bullet that by itself can sort out the problem of malaria. [However,] we believe a malaria vaccine, . . . [even a mildly effective one] could make a huge impact."[11] The research

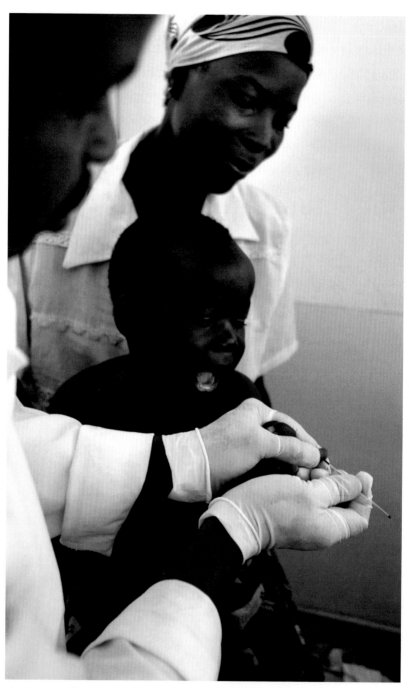

As part of a test of a very promising malaria vaccine, a doctor in Mozambique draws blood from a child.

team hopes that, after further testing, the vaccine will be ready for widespread use by 2010.

To reduce malaria in the future, governments and health officials will likely use a combination of tools. New technologies such as vaccines will join with old standards such as insecticide spraying and insecticide-treated bed nets. Education and better access to effective and low-cost treatments will play an important role. With continued research and help from developed countries and organizations such as WHO and UNICEF, there is hope for controlling malaria in the future.

Notes

Chapter 1: A Devastating Disease

1. Quoted in Lamba Simpito, "Zambia: Look Out! It's Malaria Season Again," *Times of Zambia,* October 19, 1999. http://www.malaria.org/news 121.html.

Chapter 2: The Causes and Spread of Malaria

2. Quoted in *BBC News,* "DDT and Africa's War on Malaria," November 26, 2001. http://news.bbc.co.uk/1/hi/world/africa/1677073.stm.

Chapter 3: When Malaria Strikes

3. Quoted in PBS Journey to the Planet Earth, "Stories of Hope: Nairobi, Kenya." www.pbs.org/journeytoplanetearth/hope/nairobi.html.
4. Quoted in Cathy Majtenyi, "Global Fund Highlights Malaria," *Voice of America,* November 23, 2004. www.voanews.com/english/2004-11-23-voa26.cfm.
5. Quoted in "Malaria Outbreak in Drought Affected Regions: UNICEF Provides Urgently Needed Anti-Malaria Drugs," *UNICEF Health*

Feature, August 12, 2003. www.unicef.org/ethiopia/ET_real_Malaria.pdf.

6. Nicholas D. Kristof, "Malaria Makes a Comeback, Deadlier than Ever," *New York Times*, January 8, 1997. www.malaria.org/NYTIMES.htm.

7. Quoted from Bermi, Tanzania, Web site by Peace Corps volunteer Andy Carling. http://peacecorpsonline.org/messages/messages/467/3800.html.

8. Quoted from Bermi, Tanzania Web site.

9. Quoted from Bermi, Tanzania Web site.

Chapter 4: Preventing and Treating Malaria

10. Quoted in Evans Ongwae, "Malaria Keeps Family in Poverty Cycle," *Africa Fighting Malaria,* December 2, 2004. http://news.bbc.co.uk/1/hi/world/africa/721006.stm.

11. Quoted in BBC News, "Hopes of Malaria Vaccine by 2010," October 15, 2004. http://news.bbc.co.uk/2/hi/health/3742876.stm.

Glossary

DDT: Dichloro-diphenyl-trichloroethane, an inexpensive chemical used as an insecticide.

dormant: Something that is inactive and not growing but that has the ability to become active in the future.

epidemics: Widespread outbreaks of a disease that spread more quickly than would normally be expected.

hosts: Organisms in which a parasite lives.

immunity: A body's ability to resist a particular disease.

insecticide: A chemical used to kill insects.

intravenously: Injected into a vein by way of a needle.

parasite: An organism that lives inside another larger organism, often causing harm to the larger organism.

quinine: The first effective antimalarial drug. Made from the bark of the cinchona tree native to South America.

relapse: Becoming sick again after seeming to have recovered from an illness.

vaccine: A compound given by needle or mouth that prevents a disease.

For Further **Exploration**

Books

Nancy Day, *Malaria, West Nile, and Other Mosquito-Borne Diseases.* Berkeley Heights, NJ: Enslow, 2001. This book explains how diseases are spread by mosquitoes and how to prevent being bitten. There is also a section on the future of these diseases.

Mick Isle, *Malaria.* New York: Rosen, 2001. This informative book has sections about the history of malaria as well as how it is caused, prevented, and treated. There is also a time line and a glossary.

Margy Burns Knight, *Africa Is Not a Country.* Brookfield, CT: Millbrook, 2000. This beautifully illustrated book for younger readers shows the diversity of the different countries in Africa by describing the daily life of children. It includes information about each of the 53 countries as well as pictures of their flags.

Brian R. Ward, *Epidemic.* New York: Dorling Kindersley, in association with the American Museum of Natural History, 2000. Part of the Eyewitness series, this colorful book tells about how epidemics start and spread, including malaria.

Web Sites

Centers for Disease Control and Prevention: Malaria (www.cdc.gov/malaria). This informative Web site has a wealth of information about malaria, including the history of the disease, how it is caused, and what is being done to prevent and treat it. There is also an excellent link to frequently asked questions.

Roll Back Malaria (www.rbm.who.int/cmc_upload/0/000/015/365/RBMInfosheet_8.htm). This Web site tells all about the Roll Back Malaria campaign. There is information about how malaria affects countries in sub-Saharan Africa and what is being done to control the disease.

Index

Africa
  DDT in, 11
  deaths in, 6, 23
  infection rate in, 20
  origin in, 8
  type of malaria in sub-Saharan, 21–22
  vaccinations in, 37, 39
Alonso, Pedro, 37, 39
anemia, 5
Anopheles mosquitoes, 15–17
antibiotics, 34
antimalarial drugs. See drugs
artemisinin, 34, 37
Asia, 8

Bermi (Tanzania), 26
burials, 23

cause, 9–10, 13–14
children
  deaths of, 6
  effects on, 22, 25
  exposure of, 21–22, 26
  vaccinated, 37
Chow, Jack, 22
communities
  control efforts in, 29–30
  effects on, 26–28
construction, 18–19
control. See prevention
costs
  of disease, 23, 25, 26
  of prevention, 31, 34

DDT (dichloro-diphenyl-trichloroethane)
  in cooler climates, 10
current use of, 31–33
  mosquito resistance to, 35
  sub-Saharan Africa and, 11
deaths
  in Africa, 6, 11, 23
  in Panama, 9
  from Plasmodium falciparum, 5, 13
  reducing, 31
drugs
  cost of, 23
  resistance to, 36–37
  use of, 33–34

earthquakes, 18
education, 29, 39
effects
  on children, 22
  on communities, 26–28
  on families, 23, 25, 26
  of Plasmodium falciparum, 4–5
  on pregnant women, 7, 23
eradication, 29, 37
Europe, 8

families, 23, 25, 26
"Father of Medicine, the," 12

Gorgas, William, 9–10
Greeks, ancient, 12

heat, 16–17
Hippocrates, 12
history, 7–9, 12–13
hosts, 14–15
human sweat, 16
hurricanes, 18

immunity, 21
infection rates, 6, 20
insecticides
  in cooler climates, 10
  current use of, 31–33
  mosquito resistance to, 35
  sub-Saharan Africa and, 11

Kenya, 21
Kristof, Nicholas D., 25

Laveran, Alphonse, 12

Malaria Foundation, 23
malaria parasites
  life cycle of, 14–16
  types of, 13–14
medicines. See drugs
mefloquine, 34
mosquitoes
  Anopheles, 15–17
  insecticide resistance of, 35
  in Panama, 9–10
mosquito nets, 31–32
motion, 16
Mozambique, 37, 39
Muthaka, Bernard, 31–32

natural disasters, 18
New York Times (newspaper),
  25
North America, 8

outbreaks, 17–20

Panama Canal, 9–10
Plasmodium falciparum
  deaths from, 13
  drug resistance of, 37
  effects of, 4–5
  in sub-Saharan Africa, 21–22
Plasmodium malariae, 14
Plasmodium ovale, 13–14
Plasmodium vivax, 13–14
poverty, 34
pregnant women, 6–7, 22–23
prevention
  challenges to, 19, 34–37
  methods of, 30–33, 39
  organizations working for, 29

in Panama, 10

quinine, 34

relapses, 4, 13–14
Renshaw, Melanie, 16
Roll Back Malaria (RBM), 29
Romans, ancient, 8
Ross, Ronald, 12–13

sanitation, poor, 18
smell, 16
South America, 8
spread, 8–9, 11, 12–13
Stoute, Jose, 21
sub-Saharan Africa
  DDT in, 11
  deaths in, 11, 23
  infection rate in, 20
  type of malaria in,
    21–22
symptoms
  described, 4
  development of, 15
  lack of, 14
  severity of, 20–21
  suddenness of, 6

Tanzania, 26
Tekom, Bizunesh, 25
treatment, 23, 33–34

United Nations Children's Fund
  (UNICEF), 29
United States, 10–11
University of Barcelona (Spain), 37,
  39

vaccines, 37, 39
victims, 6–7, 20–23
villages. See communities

World Bank, 29
World Health Organization
  (WHO), 10, 11, 29

Yorn, Kaiset, 25
Yorn, Yok, 25

Zulu, Christine, 6

Picture Credits

About the Author

Rachel Lynette has never had malaria. She has written several other books for KidHaven Press as well as dozens of articles on children and family life. She also teaches science to children of all ages. Lynette lives in the Seattle area in the Songaia Cohousing Community with her two children, David and Lucy; her dog Jody; and two playful rats. When she is not teaching or writing, she enjoys spending time with her family and friends, traveling, reading, drawing, rollerblading, and eating chocolate ice cream.